Hockey Goalies

Tom Greve

ROURKE PUBLISHING
Vero Beach, Florida 32964

www.rourkepublishing.com

PHOTO CREDITS: © BostjanT: Title Page; © technotr: 4, 13, 18, 19, 21, 22; © Joseph Gareri: 5, 8, 12; © Tony Tremblay: 6; © Associated Press: 7, 14, 17; © Jami Garrison: 11; © Krzysztof Zmij: 15; © Michael Braun: 16; © Dainis Derics: 20

Editor: Jeanne Sturm

Cover and page design by Tara Raymo

Library of Congress Cataloging-in-Publication Data

Greve, Tom.
  Hockey goalies / Tom Greve.
     p. cm. -- (Playmakers)
  Includes index.
  ISBN 978-1-60694-331-1 (hard cover)
  ISBN 978-1-60694-830-9 (soft cover)
 1. Hockey--Goalkeeping--Juvenile literature. 2. Hockey goalkeepers--Biography--Juvenile
literature. I. Title.
  GV848.76.G74 2010
  796.962--dc22

                                              2009006016

Printed in the USA

CG/CG

ROURKE PUBLISHING

www.rourkepublishing.com - rourke@rourkepublishing.com
Post Office Box 643328 Vero Beach, Florida 32964

Table of Contents

Goalies

Goalies have the most visible job on a hockey team. They catch or block the **puck** with their pads, sticks, or bodies so the other team won't score. Sometimes the puck comes at them incredibly fast.

Goalies are sometimes referred to as playing between the pipes. This refers to the posts, or pipes, on the goal itself.

Any shot the goalie blocks or catches is a save.

The hockey goal is made of metal posts with a mesh net attached. It is 6 feet (1.8 meters) wide and 4 feet (1.2 meters) high. The goalie plays inside a blue painted semicircle directly in front of the goal called the goal **crease.**

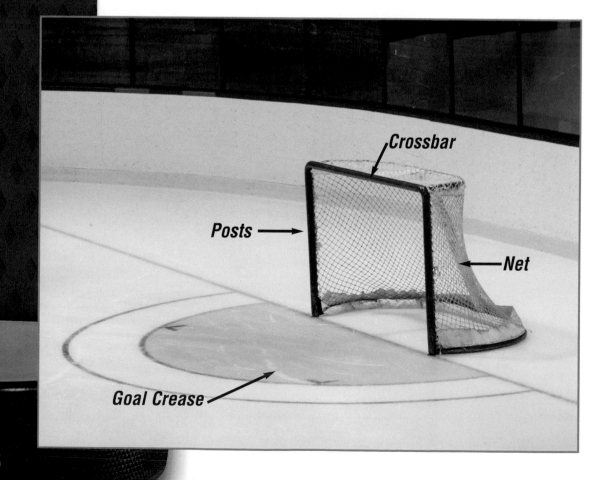

Crossbar

Posts

Net

Goal Crease

Martin Brodeur is perhaps the most accomplished current professional goalie.

Martin Brodeur has been in goal for the New Jersey Devils of the **NHL** for the past 14 years. He has won the Vezina trophy, an award given to the league's best goalie, four times. His Devils have won the **Stanley Cup** three times with him in goal. In March of 2009, Brodeur won his 552nd game as a goalie. That gave him more victories in goal than any player in NHL history. He has nearly 100 **shutout** victories.

Skills in the Crease

An effective goalie has excellent vision, balance, and quick reflexes. Goalies have to see and react to the puck constantly. This is hard to do when opponents crowd the crease looking for **rebound** shots.

Playmaker's
FACT WITH IMPACT

*Goalies play in an athletic **crouch** called the ready position. When things get crowded near the crease, they can bend their knees to get lower. This improves their line of sight on the puck. They keep their glove hand up and ready at all times.*

After making a save, the goalie must return to his ready stance immediately to be in position to block a rebound shot.

A goalie's vision allows him to see the puck and keep his body in the **shot lane.** Losing sight of the puck for even one second can leave the goalie out of position for a sudden shot on goal.

Playmaker's FACT WITH IMPACT

Despite having less ice to cover than the other players, goalies are often the best skaters on the team. As the puck moves, the goalie must also move quickly and smoothly without coming out of the ready stance. This requires quickness and balance on skates.

Playing goalie requires outstanding skating skills.

Many goalies use the butterfly style. *Butterfly saves* involve the goalie dropping to his knees and flaring his skates out to the side. The legs and stick protect the low part of the goal, while the goalie's body and hands react to high shots.

The butterfly style can leave a goalie open to pucks hit between the legs.

shot lane

The toughest puck position for goalies to protect against is straight out from the goal, since it leaves the widest shot lane to cover. As the puck goes toward the corners of the **rink,** the shot lane gets narrower.

Patrick Roy is among the greatest goalies of all time.

Patrick Roy played goalie for four Stanley Cup Champion teams during his career. He won two while playing for the Montreal Canadiens, and two more with the Colorado Avalanche. He is the only player named MVP (Most Valuable Player) in three different Stanley Cup finals. His outstanding use of the butterfly style earned him eleven NHL All-Star game appearances.

Goalies are the only players allowed to hold or freeze the puck. Freezing the puck means the goalie catches a shot in his glove or falls on a loose puck near the goal, stopping the action.

Dangers in the Crease

Playing goalie can be dangerous. A **slap shot** can sail at nearly 100 miles per hour (160 kilometers per hour). The goalie's equipment helps protect against injury.

A Goalie's Equipment:

Face Mask and Helmet

Chest Protector

Arm and Shoulder Pads

Catching Glove

Blocking Glove

Blocker Pads

Extra Skate Padding

Goalie Stick

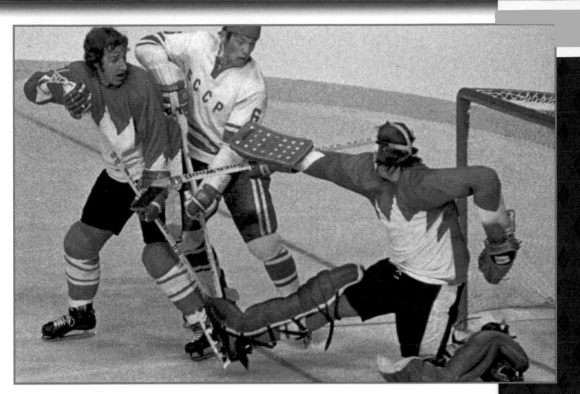

No goalie won more Stanley Cup Championships than Ken Dryden.

Hall-of-Famer Ken Dryden set an all-time record playing goalie on six Stanley Cup Championship teams in Montreal. He won five Vezina trophies. Montreal won nearly 80 percent of their games with Dryden in goal. Since retiring, Dryden won election to Canada's government.

So You Want to Be a Goalie?

Prepare for Action! Goalies have the most pressure-packed job of all the players on a hockey team. Split-second reactions make the difference between goals and saves.

When a goalie commits to one side of the net, it can leave the other side open to a quick pass and shot.

Making contact with the goalie inside the crease results in an interference penalty on the offensive player.

Playing goalie puts you in the spotlight, but it also puts you in harm's way. Offensive players attacking the net sometimes run into and over the goalie. It's a penalty, but it still hurts!

If a team is losing in the last minutes of a game, the coach sometimes replaces the goalie with a different position player leaving the goal unprotected. This is called *pulling the goalie.*

Goalies are sometimes referred to as goaltenders or netminders.

Playmaker's
FACT WITH IMPACT

Goalies use wider sticks than the other players. The extra width helps the goalie block or deflect shots.

Index

Websites to Visit

www.exploratorium.edu/hockey/save1.html
www.goalieacademy.com/articles/quotes.htm
www.nhlpa.com

About the Author

Tom Greve lives in Chicago with his wife, Meg, and their two children, Madison and William. He enjoys playing, watching, and writing about sports.